s●ul unsold

soul

unsold

photographs by Mandy Vahabzadeh

prologue by Gordon Parks   poems by Chitra Neogy–Tezak   Graystone Books, 1992

for my parents Ahmed and Mehkameh Vahabzadeh & my brothers Youssef and Bijan

for my parents Ahmed and Mehkameh Vahabzadeh & my brothers Youssef and Bijan

prologue

Intermittently in the flow of art there emerges one with an extraordinary visual sense and profound sensitivity to go along with it. The magnificent photographs of Mandy Vahabzadeh bear proof of this. It becomes immediately clear that she is not in the least self-serving, and that her true purpose is to convey understanding for her subjects – men, women and children who cover themselves with grace and dignity, even when adversity hangs over their shoulders. Only a glint in the eye sometimes hints of the turmoil smouldering inside. They seem to stare at the viewer through windows they find impossible to close, but with a presence of something indestructable about them – as if making hope together through MandyVahabzadeh's unobtrusive eye. And what one could perceive to be darkness dawns into light emboldened by pride.

Often talent such as Mandy Vahabzadeh's abides by rules set by others. But her individualism sets her apart, simply because she follows her own convictions. One looks at her photographs sensing that they are full of certainties and reasons, and there is a thirst for seeing more. They go as far as images can go without actually speaking. She appears to have acquired the freedom to master herself, and obviously she became free the moment she chose to be.

Chitra Neogy-Tezak's verse moves gracefully in the light of the photographs. It too is thickly sown with understanding – not attempting to explain Ms. Vahabzadeh's works but certainly being of significant use to them. Consequently the result brings us a lovely marriage of images and words dropped superbly and softly into place, and soul unsold becomes a testament to what many of us are, or what we have been.

Gordon Parks

when India softly speaks to me

        I wander where I used to be

a beginning in reflection
the journey . . . a child
sweet lotus story
your soul unsold

cradled in my new dream state

I watch the lake become the sky

I sip my story

and gently awake

a quiet secret

at first day break

withered grass

faded green

gentle lady

weathered dream

sitting at lands end

here sea meets sea

and sun meets sky

here waters breathe ether

and man moves center

when school is over   and lines are learnt

                              we break our boundaries

of do's and don'ts

                                   we set in motion

                                   a man-child play

                                        we fly our kites of sky and mind

                                             we take our freedom

                                                  we quietly run

a wave of wild and rapture bold
a thunder light breaks through the dark
a dawn of eyes
a birth in race
the silver tree
your shadow free

he came to tell me through my night

that I was special

that I had seen

I came to water true and clear

to be my mirror

to break my fear

walking through my mind of self

I saw a man with seed of tree

he came from gardens built in clouds

he said the goddess watched us proud

he said that he and I were incense burnt

from our palace of cracked clay

our stories unfold in a hidden way

we are the children of night and day

we live on earth and dream in sky

शान्ति निवास

my soul so straight   I hold and wait   I working man   a slow strong plan

my dreams are echoes of
the dream voice within me
dreams are my power

dreams

make

me

whole

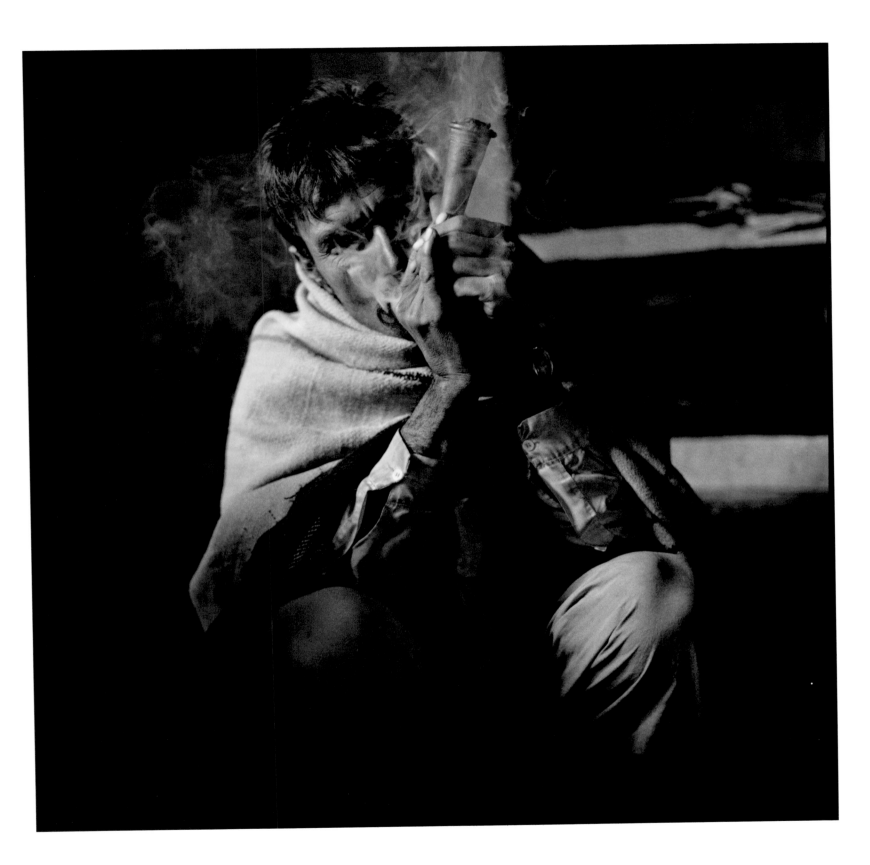

my mother is waiting

for us to come in
my brother and me
we wait for that day
traveling lady please enter and stay
she will tell us a story
of Krishna and glory

take time to dream
take time to long
don't rush and run
don't force the song

when I sit by my mother love

I hold my fears and see them run

no empty shadows near me come

she plays with earth and speaks to wood

she takes my dreams and paints them true

I throw ashes at all laws

made by man or God

I am born alone

I have no companion

I never traveled far and wide

I come to bathe at light of dawn

and in the water

soft and silk

I feel the earth

I know the stars

I now go on
I take my own
never forget me
never not see me

in remembrance   Satyajit Ray

Mandy Vahabzadeh

Of Persian origin, Mandy Vahabzadeh was born and raised in Switzerland. She came to New York to study design at Pratt Institute and later studied photography at Parsons School of Design. The Hasselblad portraits in soul unsold **were taken during prolonged stays in Kashmir, Rajasthan, Kerala, Varanasi and other rural and tribal areas in India between 1989 and 1991. Ms. Vahabzadeh currently resides in New York City.**

photo by Motoe Shiratori

Gordon Parks

One of the most important photographers of the twentieth century, Gordon Parks is something of a renaissance man, being also a renowned writer, director and composer. His critically acclaimed photographs have been collected by major art institutions and his photography books include Moments Without a Proper Name **and** A Poet and his Camera. **His autobiography,** Voices in the Mirror **was recently published, and in 1988 he was awarded the National Medal of Art.**

Chitra Neogy-Tezak

Born in Calcutta, she studied at the school founded by Tagore, the Santiniketan School for Dance and Drama, and later graduated from the Royal Academy of Dramatic Arts in London. An actress in feature films, television and theatre, in the 1980s Ms. Neogy-Tezak turned her attention to filmmaking and has written and directed numerous documentaries.

grateful acknowledgments to

Above all, my brother Youssef for being the first to express his faith in me when I took up photography.

Susan Martin for her enthusiastic backing of this work and, along with G. Ray Hawkins, for giving me a chance to be published.

Gordon Parks for his support and generosity in writing the prologue for this book.

Chitra Neogy-Tezak for her inspired response to my photographs.

Marika van Adelsberg for capturing the essence of this work in her beautiful design.

William Greaves for so kindly introducing me to Gordon Parks.

Ira Mandelbaum at Scope Associates/NYC for the fine quality of his printing.

Motoe Shiratori	Leonard Langman	Cristina Mc Ginniss
Muriel Peters	Yasmine Djerradine	Edgar Neogy-Tezak
Elyzabeth Aubert	Marina Kitrilackis	

for their precious encouragement throughout this project.

I thank you all,

Mandy Vahabzadeh

The first edition of soul unsold **is limited to 5,000 casebound copies printed on Kashmir with hand made Ginshenshi red end sheets.**

edited by **Susan Martin**

photographs copyright **Mandy Vahabzadeh, 1992**

poems copyright **Chitra Neogy-Tezak, 1992**

this edition copyright **Graystone Books, 1992**

design by **Marika van Adelsberg of 2D3D**

printed and bound by **Stinehour Press**

for

Graystone Books, 1992

520 Washington Boulevard

Suite 109

Marina Del Rey, California

90292

310. 577.7683

ISBN# 0-9630570-3-0